Classic Elements of Nature

Earth, Air, Water and Fire

(a collection of poems)

by Margaret Lee Morgan

Contents

Earth

Water

Thank you from Nature

Voice of the Current

Life Ring (keep you afloat)

The River Fish

Emotional Tides

Medicine of Water

Swimming in the Sea

Puddles of Paws

Lovely, Little Monster

An Easter Holiday

River, Spring Song

Unusual Happily Ever After

Tidal Wave

Heartbreak: Treading Water

Leakages (resulting in a flood)

Stalking Waves

Lie Detector Lake

Crying over Spilt Water

Wedding Monsoon

Deep Sea Ghosting

Fire

The Ember

Hug of a Weapon

Burning Revenge and Desire

Burning Choas

A Violent Performance

The Bird with the Burning Wings

Fire Dances

A Fierce Ruler

"The Earth has music for those who listen."

William Shakespeare

Nature's Care

The planet Earth.
The oldest song.
You are the home for generations
In the years to come.
Trees in forests breathe
As the meadows sigh.
You are a spiritual presence
Where mountains reside...
A solid base.
And a cradle of rest
Where seeds are planted
Within an ancient bed.

Bones of the Past

The truth about history:
It's buried deep,
Upturning rocks, and stones.
Snow upon mountains creates echoes.
If you were there,
You would have heard the sound
Waves
Travelling at top speed;
Incredibly fast.
The ground sits.
Completely patient,
Completely frozen,
And completely still
Until someone unearths treasures.

Earth Wins the Race

The spirit of nature is lined up here.
The gun goes off.
The race begins
Approaching the finish line.
The Earth begins screaming...
"I win. I win."
The shouts repeated in celebration.
The other runners aren't so happy.
Some have had enough.
As the winner continues celebrating...
"I win. I win."
The shouts continue to echo wildly.
It's been a while since the winners.
Notice they're on the field alone.

Bees Liquid Gold

The scents of hundreds of flowers,
The butterflies and the bees
Hang around for hours.
The bees buzz
As they all start working...
Jumping from each flower, collecting
pollen.
The worker bees carry the cargo.
Other bees produce the honey:
The edible liquid gold.

The Caterpillar

A caterpillar rests on a leaf,
Chewing away
And preparing for a long sleep.
It is warm and snug.
The caterpillars had a feast.
Sharing a table with local snails and
slugs.
Time passes as the caterpillar
Sleeps in a snug
While returning to the sunlight.
The caterpillar has had enough
Showing off its brand-new clothes,
Able to fly like never before.

World Adventures

I've travelled all over the globe:
Different sights
Different smells
Different experiences
And different gifts
Coming from different gifts
Getting a taste of the place,
I hope to return in the years to come.
I travel by road.
Travel by air.
Travel by Ocean.
It doesn't matter.
One day, I'm going anywhere
and everywhere...
Meeting new people.
Meeting many communities.
Travelling by road,
Travelling by air
And across the sea.

Nevertheless, I want to travel.
Despite people being homebodies.

Woodland

A woodland floor:
The sight of snowdrops.
A forest crowded with acorns.
A forest where squirrels are racing,
And digging up the ground,
Frantically finding their nuts.

This is a family of trees:
A display of different greenery.
Roots covered by the scenery.
Mushrooms pop up...
The most irritating fungus.

A woodland pathway
Showing the way to school.
The route seems frightening...
Getting dark earlier
During winter and fall.

The Other Side of the World

Sunshine by mid-morning...
A 24-hour flight and
it's the cold and rain.
Storms and floods.
Snowstorms
blaze on the mountains.

Tucked up in bed.
Heading off to work
Depends on where you are.

Which side of the world
are you on?

8

From Spring to Summer

Blue skies grow daffodils and snowdrops,
filling the fields and people's gardens.

Bunches of flowers transform from seeds into
the skirts of petals.
Delicate enough to be easily broken.
With the tiniest of movements.

Cherry blossoms show off brand-new colours.
More and more flowers appear.
Its development becomes competitive.
A bit like a pageant.
A rainbow spreads near and far.
The nights shrink
shorter.
The days grow warm
and longer.

Chirping sounds of the birds
fill the air in the
early hours:
Sixty minutes before
The alarm is fired.

Vacation - a Summer Holiday

Spending long days outside.
Having picnics.
Having BBQS.
Visiting the park.
Staying at the seaside.
Playing on swings or jumping waves.
Being away from home
for weeks or days.
A long weekend.
A week or a fortnight's stay.
Sightseeing.
Driving through the countryside.
Boarding a plane, boat or train.
Seeking better times...
All make the summer vacation
memorable!

Special Occasion

Special occasions like...
Birthday celebrations.
Christmas celebrations.
New Year's Eve celebrations.
Valentine's Day celebrations...
Usually, imprinting
lasting memories.

There's usually a mixture of baking,
Cooking a meal or going out
for the day.
Pancakes are cooked on Shrove Tuesday.
The lamb is roasted in the oven.
A present given with a bow.
Hearts exchanged plenty.
Rings and bracelets are given in
remembrance of a wedding.

Flowers.
Put into vases.
Placed on a grave in order
Not to forget a loved one.

Shadows

Shadows in the dark:
The forest is in the background.
A beautiful spot:
It is the local National Park.

People are parking their cars.
People are pitching their tents.
People are building campfires.
And cooking their food.

Children are toasting marshmallows,
Rolling out the sleeping bags,
And double-checking whether the fire
Hadn't continued burning.

Torches turned on and off.
Mistaking shadows for monsters.
Hiding in sleeping bags.
Reading books and comics.

Spring into Easter

The past dissolves as the soul is free.
Renewing our love for the arrival of spring.
Walking the paths where the river sings.

Easter whispers as plants arise,
April showers
are around the corner.

Failing to dampen everyone's spirits
As the whole family begins
Easter celebrations.

Buried Truths

The Earth is quiet, deep, and still...
Holding secrets hidden within the soil
As plant roots whisper.
Rumours spread all over the area.
The ground reveals the macabre answer.
Bones.
A skeleton
showing signs of murder.

The Graveyard

A garden of stone.
Where the trees keep guard.
Leaving a feeling of being enclosed.

Digging deep, you'll find the plant roots
Continuously creeping,
Feeding on the things thrown away
Such as eggshells and potato peelings.

Rotting outside as the grave's smile widens
Leaving the Earth speechless
with zero choices.

The End of the World

Deep underground,
The sea and rivers crawl,
Thick with oil and dark, almost black.
The earth drinks,
But the result isn't forthcoming.
The tree and flowers feel choked.
Rust and waste continue to smoke
Allowing large amounts of smog
Causing contamination, humanity
forever witnessed
The world attempts to start over again.
Greenhouse gases continue to spread
over the years.

Earthquake

You swallow towns.
Women and children
Were against the stone and debris.
That's when everybody is forced.

To leave their homes:
The stretch of ground where nothing lies.

The Earth cracked
Leaving bare bones and dryness.

Easy Life

The hills look strong,
And the cliffs stand high.
The perfect life you were told
Turned out to be a lie.

There is flooding in autumn and into winter.
The place is drowning with tourists.
Come the summer season.

Come the summer season.
Every day, items are a lot more expensive.
Healthcare access has become
non-existent.

The quiet life is a dream.
Is it too far?
That's to be decided.
Between your real life
And your imaginary lifestyle.

Soils Remember

When you're planting,
You're also
Building
Digging
Drilling
And paving the path
Across the fields and to popular hiking spots
Thereby getting steeper and steeper.
The land keeps a record
While you plan to make a change.
Roots have scars
Struggling with the future
Needing to bring back the past.
Much has changed.
Much has stayed the same.
Memories that nature holds
Attempting to reclaim.

Trees Disappearance

Don't forget when storms arrive.
Floods and windstorms have started to thrive.
A fallen tree in the path of the sunshine
Taken.
Stolen.
Disappeared.
Alas, the natural umbrella
It is no longer there.

"The air soft as that of Seville in April, and so fragrant that it was delicious to breathe it."

Christopher Columbus

Invisible Visitor

An unknown visitor
Was knocking secretly on doors...
Hopes
Dreams
Fears
Are carried away from the shore.
Hums so softly, so low in tone.
It's a lullaby that only.
The riverbed knows,
Helping birds fly,
Stirring up leaves and branches
That touches the clouds in the sky
Whispering over and over again.
That visitor can't be seen.
Weaving patterns of silver thread.

Cool Breeze, Bitter Wind

The Pulse of the day and the heart of the night.
A breath.
Freedom.
So swift and light.

Songs carried across dunes and sand.
The music heard across
valleys and farmers' land.

The waking of leaves,
Waving branches on trees:
A restless spirit
Speaking in another language.

Soft kisses touch children's faces:
Changing.
Developing.
Quick to bite people's fingers.

The Air's Reign

A storm is rolling in,
And it's ready to play.
The wind arrives
Before the hail and before the rain.
Restless in their mischief,
The air fuels their self-belief.

The plan begins as the sun retreats,
Racing to be first.
The wind makes an unleashed swirl.
The leaves immediately fall off the trees.

The air is turning sharper.
The sky becomes so much darker.

The rain and hail join forces,
Pouring rain, travelling faster and faster.
Droplets become stone-frozen.

The hail is released.
Hoods from raincoats pulled
Around faces and heads
Hugging tighter.
Many struggle to hold on to umbrellas.

Gusts of air join a clumsy dance
Just as quickly as the roads start flooding.

The rain has given up on the stormy scheme.
The wind steps back
Just as the hail lets out a scream.

The episode lasted half an hour.

The storm departs,
leaving a light rain shower.
Could the tempest have lasted longer?
Maybe,
But the air is now sombre.

The air and wind
Came up with another plan.
Additional rain and hail
It would have made the storm last.
Going on and on.

Sense of Oxygen

You can't grab the empty space with your fingers.
It's impossible to touch.
You can hold your arm up
for as long as possible.
There is no taste.
Perhaps, if you're in the kitchen
As somebody cooks dinner.

I can hear my breath,
There is no oxygen answering:
The one thing we all need
is disappearing.

It's hard
when you can't feel, see or smell
If oxygen is coming.

The Tornado

The alarm's activated,
And we all dash to the basement,
Bolting the door to where we keep things
In storage,
Huddling together to keep warm.
My older brother and Dad
Start dragging a chest of drawers,
Blocking the family in for safety.
The local area lost so many houses
Waiting out for the end of the storm
Shaking out dusty blankets,
To plump up Grandma's old pillows.
That's when we all realise
We'll be hiding here for a day at least.
A few hours pass as the storm turns out in force.
We would all discover later.
It was one of the worst.

Music of the Wind

The wind is singing a different tune.
Positive or negative,
We all hear the song.
It is brand new.
A change of mood

Leaves the rain running.
The sky is clearer
Leading the sunshine to jog
Right into the painting.

Voices riding on the breeze.
A cool-down from the sunshine's heat.
Nobody knew the song the wind was carrying.
The air was changing the sheet music.
As the wind approaches.

The music spreads
Across towns and cities.
All the misery is blowing away.
The community sings as they go about their business.

The music is the breath fluttering
Through the leaves
Down the river,
As I listen to the lyrics

Spreading through the local train's
steam.

The laughter from the playing children
Changes the song's tempo
As their parents chase after them.

That's a sign
That the sun is sending
In his brother.

Now, it's time for the moon to take over.
The air is still singing.
The community listens,
Paying more attention
To the music of nature.

Storm's Pranks and Games

Friends are coming together.
The sky turns dark
As the lightning starts the prank off.
The thunder joins in the game.
The scene turns from calm.
To be completely wild.
The summer weather turns to mean
and regeful.

On the beach,
The sea isn't very grateful.
The waves are giant.
The trees shake and cower from the storm
The prank clears the air.
The rain, thunder and lightning
Continue their games for about a week.

The Ghost (a Wonderer)

It drifts through trees,
It hums.
It sighs.
A shapeless whisper
A shadow in disguise.
No footprints are left in the sand.
Nobody to hold a hand.
A breeze is stirring up leaves.
Whispers and whistles
Tell a story through history.
A restless soul is making communication.
I just wanted to let you know that there's no place
to stay.
No place to call home,
the whistles are left to roam.

The Healing

The wind arrives with a gentle blow
With a breath so light.
Many fail to notice it coming down the road.
The air is so soft and sweet

Drying your tears
As it hears your footsteps,
And your weary eyes as the air clears the sky.

A sight travels through tree branches
Leaving the leaves to dance with the flowers.
No hands are touching.
No voice is speaking.
Simply, the wind generates
people's energy.

The Statue

The statues freeze in an endless stare.
The word still moves, and the air leads it...
Breathing life where stone stands still.
Curling through gaps, living its own rules.

The wind wraps closer...
Twisting
Turning
Right past the statue
Standing in silent pride.

A cold face
Of stone expects the cracks
It tries to hide.

Loved One's Spirit

A gentle voice
Speaking in times of need.
Though times has flown by,
I know you're near beside me.

A part of the sky.
Whistles.
Whispers.
Laughter is coming from the streams.
I'm convinced I see you standing
In the frame of the bathroom door.

Melodies played on the radio.
Your laughter echoes wherever I go...
The breeze in the morning.
The rainbow on the sky canvas.
And a beautiful painting.

Silent Communication

A cold day in winter.
The arrival of the night
Makes the wind spill secrets.
It's a silent form of communication.

Walking home, trying to ignore
All of the whispers.
All of the whistles.

Still, the frost is coming in
Fighting for the head of the table.
The wind gives up nothing.
The frost begins spreading.

Forever Affection

Your voice lingered in the air.
A whisper.
A prayer.
Memories you don't always wish to share
Though time has pulled you out of sight.
The wind calls you
Very late all night

Pulling on my ponytail.

The touch is gentle.
I feel a coolness on my skin.
It might turn out to be nothing.
In my words, it means a lot.
That gust of wind
Equals forever love.

Travelling the Wind

I had utterly lost the motivation.
Can't understand it.
I'm thinking of a rocket launch.

Swept away by the wind in the early hours,
I didn't chase it.
I stared at the ceiling
Before turning out the light.

The wind is twisted,
Chewed and spat out.
My confidence positively has been destroyed.
Anxiety and depression can speed up.
Or slow down.

The pressure of life can ride the wind.
It can take a holiday
Before it returns.
The panic will likely begin again.

Voices

The secrets are many.
The sound is so clear.
"You're a mess.
Did you remember to brush your hair?"
The letters and words of
Voices not seen
Are always heard
Telling you, "Don't bother getting out of bed."
Useless body, you feel
You can't do anything.
The voices scream aloud, "FAILER!"
Even with energy in the tank,
You can't pick yourself back up again.
The voices are loud.
The voices are quiet.
The voices are never, ever silent.

The World's Inside

Empty head:
An open window letting in drafts,
Filling the brain with utter dread
Knocking left
Knocking right
In the ears, ringing out "Worthless."

Seemingly,
The voice
The wind
Understood the words
Filling the skulls with dust.

Echoes continue their calls.
Panic arises.
The wind, the breeze is setting in...

The cause of pushing friends and family away.
Positive
And negative
Thoughts always arise
In a particular way
After the clouds.

Negativity floats away,
Watching the clouds drift,

Returning the next day
Light and fluffy

Reaching out to catch...
Swearing.
Laughing.
Your whispers hurt,
And I'm the punching bag.

Pity?
I do not want sympathy from anyone.
Looking up, my eyes chase the clouds
In every single direction.

Wind's Short Memory

Whispering...
Slipping in between...
A name heard beneath the breeze.
Secrets riding.

Lost being spun around.
Knowing with every breath
Makes a harmonic sound.

Treading carefully,
Not even speaking.
Remember the wind
Never forgets.

But the wind's memory
Has always been short-term.
Anything long-term is history.

Choking on Promises

The air was fresh.
The sky is so clear.
Factories are rising
And increasing every year.
A change is happening.
Vows pledge a new beginning.
Yet, there's meddling.
Change causes defeat many times over.
It is extremely common.

The Vanishing Act

The air is quiet,
Light and free
Drifting away.
Always having
Somewhere to be.
Filling our lungs.
Shaping our wings.
Playing pranks on the clouds.
Chooses the moment to sing softly.
Then suddenly roars extremely loud.
Sometimes ignored leaving
everything unclear.
Nobody noticed the wind (the air).
It isn't here.

"Water is the mirror of nature."

Saint Francis of Assisi

Thank You from Nature

"Thank you," says the river.
It continues running free.
Carrying ripples of dreams.
Living locally.

"Thank you," says the ocean.
Providing gems from the salty sea.

The waves provide treasure.
Sand and pebbles scratch your feet,
Getting stuck between your toes,
Overflowing your shoes,
Making it very difficult
To walk along the shore.

"Thank you," says the raindrops
Dancing on my skin.
A raincoat keeps you warm.
Sheltered by an umbrella.
Or standing under a tree's branches.

"Thank you," whispers the water

Whether it's from the streams or the storms.

"Thank you," I say.

You give me health,

Keep me away from dehydration:
A problem I had dealt with years before.

Voice of the Current

The river kept shouting directions.
"Go left. Go right."
My kayak is obeying.

I was a deer in the headlights.

"Watching out for the rocks!"
I thought I heard someone scream.
It's a bit too late
As my boat and paddles
Break in front of me.

The current is laughing.
It's the story of the day.
I fell into the river.
Now, I'm without a boat.
I swim to the banks
And walk away.

"You are a silly sailor."
I thought I heard as I leave.

Life Ring (Keep you Afloat)

I will be by your side.
I will be there, keeping you floating;
Praying that you are still alive.
I will keep you afloat.
I will be launched.

I am your lifeboat.
I will pull you to shore.
I will help you with healing.

We know we are each other's cure.
I will keep on swimming.
I will bring you home.
We will freeze from the water.
Yet, you don't arrive.
You're left sinking like a stone.

The River Fish

A king of the streams
Swimming up and down the currents,
Chasing the fins in the tail.
Life's a dream.
Glaring at the ducks and swans
Swimming passed;

Forever running away
From a fisherman's
Hook and rod,
Forgetting the places
The rod had been cast in before.

The fish has lived
In the river, the longest.
His throne is a rock.
His crown is a weed
Found in rivers and ponds.

Emotional Tides

An endless sea and soul are free.
People are feeling.
People are dreaming.
People are spending ages weeping.

The current is deep,
Carving stone down to nothing...
Steaming, sighing, bending,
breaking, swaying
And guiding the way straight into the sea.

A silver thread is singing in my dreams.
The waves and rivers refuse to hide.
The strongest feelings and emotions
Are getting locked inside.

Medicine of Water

I'm not sure my bladder can take much more.
A remedy,
Simple,
Yet pure.
Drinking glass after glass
It might be a benefit to your health.
What people don't tell you.
You'll spend all your time on the toilet.
Drinking water fixes headaches.
Drinking water fixes heartache.
Drinking water is a great medicine.
It's an antibiotic,
But it will have you sprinting to the loo
Every thirty minutes.

Swimming in the Sea

The tide is moving as I rise.
Things are happening,
Leaving no trace.

I'm caught by surprise
Adapting myself to fit into place.
A deep love.
A deep fear.

Freezing every feature of my face.

Disappearing...
A storm is returning,
Feeling a bit calmer.
But I'm still to this day a worrier.

I don't always show it.
I don't exactly like it.
I get soaked in the restless waves.

Puddles of Paws

A life with our pets...
A delightful flaw.
A mess of pure joy.
Soaking wet
With your pet's claws
Soaking wet
Through my shoes
Splashed by paws
From a lot of puddles.
Splashes of love.
Paws dancing with glee.
Every step
Another wet patch for me to clean.
A cat with a flick of the tail.

Loving, Little Monster

A love of exploring.
The hatred of water is a
Difficult relationship.
Having a soul for adventures,
Shaking all four paws
As you walk through puddles
Again and again
Cuddling a hot water bottle
Playing with pieces of string
Getting yourself in a muddle.
Someone's crying.
The tears have started.
You give a paw.
You are the medicine
For the brokenhearted.
Right at my side,
Before you run wild.

An Easter Holiday

A sign from Grace
A loving light;
Several waves arrive.

Shades of gold fill hearts...
Delightful.
Joyous laughs.

Here comes Easter Sunday celebrations.
The tide reacts,
Then quickly vanishes.

Praying for a safe arrival...
The family gather around
As chocolate eggs are being hunted.

Easter festivities...
The party continues for longer.
The memories leave a damp,
sandy trail,
Footprints, paws, and soggy wet tails.

River, Spring Song

Flowing rivers where sorrow once stood.
The arrival of spring
Uplifts everyone and everything.
By the river,
Flowers are awoken
To the arrival of spring.
Petals are in the current swimming.
Early morning ice is now melting.
The hums of the birds in the early hours
And the whistles are gradually getting louder
and louder.
Ducks and swans are swimming
As the days get longer and warmer

Unusual, Happily Ever After

Sailing away together,
Our love is deeper
As the tidal waves keep rolling...
Through storms.
Through sunshine.
Through pouring rain.
Through calm and rough tides.
No journey is the same.

Swear you would love me forever.
Swear I'm cheating on you
With a friend of your brother.

I'm swearing I'll never betray you.
Down by the ocean
On the shore alone
Five years on
From the day we got together
Bobbing along
Alone at sea.

I'm not in a boat.
Instead, I'm on a raft.
You would have saved me from drowning.
Instead, I stay afloat.

As time rolls on,
It was you out there waiting.
You cradled me.
You kept me warm.

Who would have thought
Eight years on
We'd still be engaged.
A year later,

Married at the local Town Hall.
All the bonds came from sailing on the ocean together.
Been through angry tides,
We've spent time in glorious weather.

Tidal Wave

You were the ocean:
Vast and wild.
I was a fool:
A love-struck
Passive child.
The sea pulls me in
Deeper than ever:
A fast tidal wave
at the time
Couldn't have been any better.

Heartbreak: Treading Water

Now, I am to tread water alone.
I am left in
The sea,
The ocean,
Gasping
Fighting
And swallowing water.
I am struggling for survival
For my love and my feelings
Who is holding me tightly?
So, I try to continue floating.
The rips of the sea that I'm riding.

I feel as though I'm stuck.
In nature's washing machine.
It isn't the sharks.
It isn't the jellyfish.
It is the power of nature
That gives me fear
That gives me dread
Even a rock pool is growing inside my head.

Leakages (the result of a flood)

At first, it dripped
Now and then.
Doubts have recently crept up again.
Ignoring the emotions,
Until the flood arrives.

Sweet words were spoken,
But I pushed them aside.
The flood and my ignorance
Have done plenty of damage.

Possessions are stolen.
The feelings are different.
The rain starts pouring again
Leaving family and friendships
Ending in tears;
Calling repeatedly for a plumber.
Hopefully, calling to repair my heart
full of fear.

Stalking Waves

Notes are sent from across the channel.
The messages are found.
Those are sent within a bottle.

Then, more notes arrived
From an anonymous sender.
Then you turned up.
A wave was almost
knocking me over.

I loved you once years ago.
That was the truth.

I didn't end it.

That was you.

Like a surfer riding a wave,
You sent me love notes
Turning up at the house
During the night or day.

Simply stood across the road,
Staring for hours:
Perhaps even days.
You were busy sending paper.

Through the letterbox
Forever branding me a liar.
The waves continue
Crashing at my door.
You caused a flood
Because I was dumped.
Now, you want me back,
But you're now being rejected
Leaving your heart
Swollen and sore.

The messages keep coming.
I don't care about the words.
I don't care about your language.
You refuse to stop the sea from flooding.

It was a nice feeling at the start.
Feeling the puddles of deep water
Surrounding my feet and ankles.

Now, I dread it.
I fear the sound from the letterbox
You refuse to stop
The crash of the waves.
Continue again.
Over and over.

Lie Detector Lake

The love was smooth.
It's a lake of glass.
The water's calm.
The water's pure
Stretching out so vast,
Stepping into deep water.

Is it a trap?

The lake is a law unto itself.
The lies will soon be unravelled.
Leaving a lair
Completely tangled within the water
Crawling onto the banks, soaked.

Crying over Spilt Water

There is no use crying
When your heart is protected.
The full cup of water,
The glass is cracked and damaged.

It was a slip of carelessness.
The grip was loosened by emotional turmoil...

Dripping wet.
Spilling water.
Droplets carving pure devotion
Making a decision.

The relationship is over.
Stop your crying.
It will be alright.
You'll find the right partner.
Let's clean up the water.

Wedding Monsoon

We said I do down by the ocean.
It was a perfect day at the seaside.

Standing on the shore,
There's the groom.
The bride is being walked down the aisle.
The vows exchanged
Down by the waves
Crashing as a wave breaks
Increasing in size.

We all realise this has been a mistake
Trying to surf or catch a wave;
Trying to stay afloat.
Fear is what remains.
The monsoon
Has taken the party's place.

Deep Sea Ghosting

Your love was deep,
And your words were kind
Like the tide.

You had quickly changed your mind.

One day you're here.
The next, there's no trace.
You're gone,
Disappeared in a single wave.

Now sitting alone at the water's edge,
I wish the two of us
Had been swept away instead.
We went our separate ways.
This is our life:
A dramatic change.

"One must never let the fire go out in one's soul, but keep it burning."

Vincent van Gogh

The Ember

It sleeps in ash so small.
So bright.
A quiet glow.
A hidden light.
Waiting with patience.
Breathing softly and slowly.
In a fiery glory.
A spark.
A flicker.
The fire wakes.
Dancing flames.
The heat overtakes.
It's small yet,
Don't be fooled.
Look at the damage.
It's small yet,
Don't be fooled.
Look at the damage.
It's right behind.
You were there.
You stayed completely silent.

Hug of a Weapon

A burning heart that never stops:
fierce deadly weapon
Causing warmth and screams
Making people shout.

A gentle flame
Keeping everyone warm
With shy sparks
Developing into another form.

Anger burning
Secrets uncovered
Running deeply.
The pulse of the stories
Perhaps too wild.

Jealousy too burns
Creating serious damage
As a flamethrower
Provides total wreckage.

Burning Revenge and Desire

The source of destruction:
The guide to those we remember.
A dancer of shadows
Using the flames of many embers.

Then, sparklers bring laughter.
Also, whispers of the darkest rumours...
Revenge.
Desire.
A photograph of ash and fumes:
A toxic mixture.

Burning Chaos

Fire crackles, burning bright.
Orange and blue sparks
Are dancing through the night.
The growing heat intensifies
Feeding on wood
Releasing the black smog.
Embers reach before an explosion
begins swirling
The roof caves in as the fire begins playing.

The smoke consumes every house feature
As quickly as the game started.
The embers then gradually begin cooling.

The fire sighs,
"I guess it's bedtime."
The flame's work is completed.
The heat thins as the smog stands defeated.

A Violent Performance

Taking a curtsey,
The flames perform an ecore.
A terrified audience stays still
As the windows burst.
The fire is finishing its performance.

Act One involved
The collapse of the staircase.
The flames had a feeding frenzy.
In Act Two, a flamethrower appeared.
Turning the stairs to ash already.
The windows smashed into so many pieces.
The scenery: the set is burnt to the ground.
Smoke and char were the only things
People could smell.

A completed show...
But the audience doesn't clap.
The audience doesn't cheer.
The people stand there
In complete shock, staring and crying.

The Bird with the Burning Wings

"Beware of the bird with the burning wings."
At the centre of famous tales,
Myths and legends,
Sparks turning a flight into a barbecue.

The bird's reflection in the mirror
Would be a shock to either one of you.

Ignoring the smoke
Coming from his tail
As he flapped his wings,
His feathers started to sizzle.

Who would have thought
The bird was a danger to the sky.
Simply a bird with goals and ambitions
That was out of his reach.
They were far too high.

Fire Dances

In life and death,
Both are forces of light and nature.
It's a fierce relationship...
A warm embrace.
The cause of damage.
The fuel of dreamers.
Shaping the past and directing the future.

Flames are constantly dancing.
Restless sparks are growing more manic.
As it takes more risks and more chances.

A Fierce Ruler

A king.
A queen.
Claiming a stubborn lead.
A force is calling.
Yet, the leadership
Determines responsive answers.
A leader, bold and bright,
Carving a reign ending with a match.
The blaze gradually gets taller,
Breaking up the stars
Appearing one by one in the night.

Nightmare Campfire

The log complains to the great oak:
"The fire's burning fast."
The oak witnesses the grin.
"I'll have a blast."
The fire screams...
Sending snaps, crackles, and pops
Forcing the oak tree to get out of the way
With a lean of the branches.

As the whole forest starts paying attention,
The tears of the fire go crazy and manic.
Golden drops fall
While the forest mourns
The fire's damage
"All because of a campfire
Wasn't put out correctly."
The log said to speak up.
The whole forest watched
As the smog rose up to the rooftops.

The Garden's Past

The garden sighs,
And the air is dry.
The fire appears all of a sudden.

As the fire leaps,
It is because it is higher and higher.
Flowers and trees begin to scream.
The flames ignore the shouting and pleas,
Consuming the area with smoke and ash.

That coming spring,
The flowers bloom all over again.
It's a natural method to press the restart.
The fire has cleared the garden's past.

What's left now is a brand new-beginning
And a brand-new start.

The Sun's Side Hustle

The sun instructs, the fire of rays
Commanding "burn and let the ice melt
As you play your games."

The flames yawn, stretching tall.
"I won't play any games on your behalf."

The rays opened their eyes.
Upon making an answer.

There's a moment of silence.
The sunshine's warmth
Floated just above the ground.
"Guess I'd better warm up the world."

Working together,
The sunshine's warmth
Floated just above the ground.
"Guess I'd better warm up the world."

Working together,
The sun, rain, and wind
Provide warmer weather
Burning standing in the direct line of fire.

Soon, the sun tiers.
The heatwave is over.
An increase in work begins.
At the end of the season.
The sun's work decreases.
It'll pick up again before
Anybody knows it.

Cookout

The forest's chef,
The flames are in charge.
Grilling the pine cones,
Either small or large;
Toasting the seeds
As the trees dress the wood for dinner.

The forest knows it's good.
Thanks to the smell
Carried by the weather.
A meal was eaten,
And the guests are full.
Clearing up has started
Before the sight of the moon.

Thunder and Lightning's Idea

Lightning struck and grinned with glee:
"Let's start a fire."
Cheering to the thunder,
"You and me."
The grass grasped the trees,
Which stood tall.
"Great," said Lightning.
"The flames will eat
The garden whole."
Little shoots and grass turned around.
That's when the lightning strikes.
Wandering off,
The thunder didn't back down.
Eventually, it grew tired,
Spinning around,
And making a quick retreat.

Screaming Ashes

The forest burned.
Such a hungry beast
Now turning secrets
Into animals eating at a feast.

A boy is lost,
But his skeletal bones
Were eventually found
Completely charred.

A crime has been committed.
Police,
Detectives,
Forensics,
And everybody was working hard
To solve a case of murder.

Lanterns of an Arsonist

A midnight sky,
Licked with red.
A log cabin glowing
As the wood's thoughts
Turn to dread.

The fire is spreading.
It's only caught by chance.
It all began
With a tiny spark.

In the coal,
The truth is silent.
A mistake.
A slip-up.
A misstep in a dance.

The house is still standing.
Just minutes ago,
The property ablaze:
Continuously burning.

Hunting

The match was struck,
And a deal was made.
The fire danced,
And a debt was paid.
No fingerprints,
Not even a single clue:
Just smoke and cinders.
A fire's breath is in front of you.
Inside is death itself.
A complex investigation is needed
To track down criminals
For no time can be wasted.

Ashes Snitching

A barn is ablaze.
The glow is noticed
In the distance.
Residents and animals
Are left crying.
The result is whispers
And the glow witnessing the ember.
The farmer is heard swearing.
"Just an accident?"
People are lying.
The wind is shifting.
The ashes have only
Just started talking.

Song of Arson

The trees in the woods are glowing.
The sky causes the alarm to start screaming.

The flames bury dreams.
The smoke is taking away.
Any plans and schemes?

Turning on a light
In the early hours
In the middle of the night
Witnesses first discovered the fire,
Only to see a spark.
The smog turns the sky.
To pitch, black, dark.

Fierce the fire has become.
Having completed the damage,
It fails to destroy the evidence
Held by the stars and the moon.

Funeral by Fire

No coffin is too deep.
No grave is too hard to dig.
Fire is burning uncontrollably.
Sweeping away a lot of secrets.

Information is a rewritten story.
The flames are at the centre of the action.

The results of the burning
Wipe out the future.
The happenings left in devastation.

Cinders Cried

The field ignites.
The bush burns so bright...
A flicker.
A spark.
A night of destruction.
The fire starter was like the Tinman
From the Wizard of OZ.

They didn't have a heart.
They didn't care about the harm.
A massive fire was spreading from field to field.

Some remains look as though
They could smolder forever.

Bibliography

Koch, N. (March 01st, 2021). 21 Inspiring Quotes on the Air Element. Mandala Mind. Available at:www.mandalamind.org>blog>21-inspiring-quotes-on-the-air-element [7th March 2025].

Koch, N. (March 01st, 2021). 21 Inspiring Quotes on the Earth Element. Mandala Mind. Available at:www.mandalamind.org>blog>21-inspiring-quotes-on-the-earth-element [8th March 2025].

Koch, N. (March 01st, 2021). 21 Inspiring Quotes on the Fire Element. Mandala Mind. Available at:www.mandalamind.org>blog>21-inspiring-quotes-on-the-fire-element [Accessed 4th March 2025].

Systrom & Krieger, Kevin & Mike. Instagram. Meta Platforms, Inc., 2010. Available at:www.instagram.com>asinglebeing [Accessed 14 April 2025].

Keep in touch

@descriptionson_fiction

@FictionDescript

@descriptionson_fiction

@TravelWatch_Review &
@Descriptionsonfiction

Email
descriptionsonfiction@gmail.com

Author Newsletter Coming Soon

LOVE
& LIFE

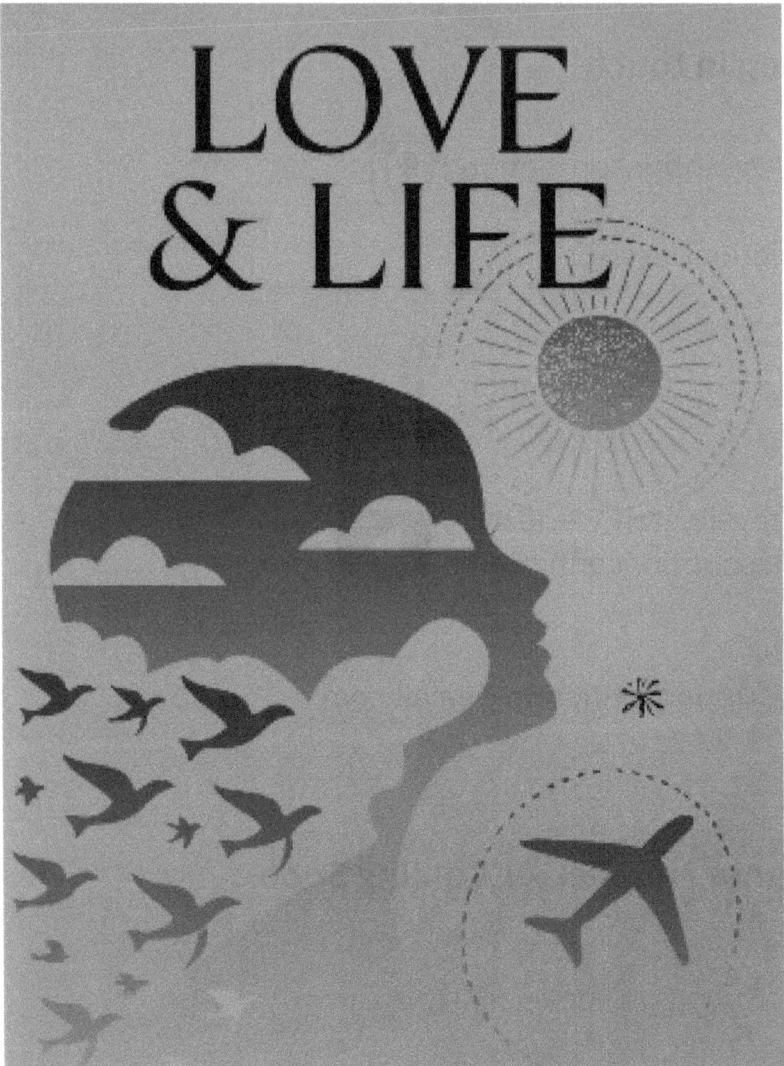

Acknowledge ments

Creating Classic Elements of Nature has been a challenging, personal journey for me as an adult, a writer, and a poet. While writing all these poems, I spent the day in London, stayed a week in the hospital, and seriously broke my left leg.

Upon writing the page in question, I've just passed week eight, so it's been two months since I had surgery. Reflecting on the classic four elements of nature—Earth, Air, Water, and Fire—was a much-needed reflection. I first need to acknowledge my excellent editor for pointing out the mistakes that Grammarly missed and for giving me the best feedback yet. Your guidance brought clarity and the required refinement. Let's hope this isn't the last time I'm pleased with the feedback.

My family and friends have been amazing and have always supported me with my writing. As I write my second poetry collection, I'm grateful to all my friends who reached out as soon as they learned what happened in February 2025. Thank you for all your messages and well wishes.

I need to say a massive thank you to all my relatives, particularly on my Dad's side. Many travelled down to see me during that week in a hospital in London when Mum couldn't make the train journey. Things would have been a lot harder without your continuing support. Plus, I can not forget the family cat, Coco, who forever offers comfort, inspiration, and paws of ideas.

The voices of nature itself—the rustling trees, the flowing rivers, the candle flames, and the whispering winds—have inspired the poems within these pages. It means I need to pay attention to the wonders outside the front door and beyond.

Finally, many thanks to all of you, the readers. I still need to pinch myself every day that people read my books and poems.

I hope to continue this.

www.ingramcontent.com/pod-product-compliance
Lightning Source LLC
Chambersburg PA
CBHW050545280326
41933CB00011B/1724